Novena Devotion to St. Joseph

Prayer that Never Fails

Rev. Sr. Immaculata

Dedication

To All Catholics in the World

This book is dedicated to all Catholics around the globe who, with unwavering faith and devotion, have embraced St. Joseph as a powerful intercessor and a beloved patron. Your love for St. Joseph and your commitment to deepening your relationship with him inspire and encourage us all.

May this book serve as a source of knowledge, inspiration, and spiritual nourishment as you continue to grow in your devotion to St. Joseph. May it strengthen your faith, ignite your love for God and the Holy Family, and guide you in experiencing the everlasting power of the Novena to St. Joseph.

In your unwavering commitment to the Catholic faith, you are a beacon of light and hope in the world. As you honor St. Joseph and seek his intercession, may his fatherly love and protection be with you, guiding you on your journey of faith.

May St. Joseph, the silent guardian of the Holy Family, intercede for you and your loved ones, and may his example of faith, humility, obedience, purity, and patience inspire you to live lives of holiness and virtue.

With heartfelt gratitude for your dedication and fervor, this book is lovingly dedicated to all Catholics in the world.

May God bless you abundantly on your spiritual journey.

Amen.

Table of contents

Introduction

Saint Joseph, the foster father of Jesus and the chaste spouse of the Blessed Virgin Mary, holds a special place of honor and reverence in the hearts of millions around the world. Throughout the ages, his steadfast faith, humility, and unwavering commitment to God's divine plan have made him a beloved figure within the Catholic Church and beyond. In this book, we embark on a journey to explore the significance of St. Joseph and the profound impact his intercession can have on our lives.

From the very beginning, St. Joseph's role in salvation history was extraordinary. Chosen by God to be the earthly guardian of the Son of God, he embraced this divine mission with unwavering devotion and trust. Although often depicted in the background of the Nativity scene, St. Joseph's silent strength and deep faith played a vital part in the unfolding of God's plan for humanity.

As the patron saint of fathers, workers, and the Universal Church, St. Joseph holds a special place as a model of virtue and holiness. His humble obedience to God's will, even in the face of great uncertainty, serves as an inspiration to all believers. St. Joseph's exemplary life teaches us the value of humility, selflessness, and trust in God's providence.

In recent years, the devotion to St. Joseph has experienced a resurgence within the Church. Pope Francis declared the Year of St. Joseph, acknowledging his profound influence and encouraging the faithful to seek his intercession and follow his example. Through this renewed devotion, countless individuals have experienced the power of St. Joseph's prayers and witnessed the miracles and graces obtained through his intercession.

The novena devotion to St. Joseph is a time-honored tradition that has been cherished by believers for centuries. By engaging in focused prayer over a period of nine days, we open ourselves to receive St. Joseph's guidance, protection, and intercession in our lives. This powerful spiritual practice allows us to draw closer to this beloved saint, seeking his assistance in various aspects of our lives, including family life, work, personal struggles, and spiritual growth.

In this book, we explore the depth and significance of the novena devotion to St. Joseph. We delve into his virtues, his role in salvation history, and his special patronage over various aspects of our lives. Through personal testimonies and stories of miraculous intercession, we witness the profound impact of St. Joseph's prayers in the lives of believers.

Whether you are seeking comfort, guidance, or spiritual growth, the devotion to St. Joseph offers a pathway to deepen your relationship with God. As we embark on this journey together, may the pages of this book serve as a source of inspiration and encouragement, inviting you to embrace the powerful intercession of St. Joseph and experience the transformative power of his prayers in your life.

Open your heart and allow the love of St. Joseph to guide you, for his intercession truly is a prayer that never fails.

Chapter 1: Discovering the Power of the Novena

- The History and Significance of Novenas

The practice of novenas has been deeply rooted in the traditions of the Catholic Church for centuries. In this chapter, we delve into the history and significance of novenas, shedding light on the power and efficacy of this devoted form of prayer. By understanding the roots and purpose of novenas, we can better appreciate the transformative potential they hold in our spiritual lives.

Novenas trace their origins to the early Christian Church, where believers would gather for nine consecutive days of prayer leading up to significant feast days or special intentions. The word "novena" itself is derived from the Latin word "novem," meaning "nine." This period of focused prayer allows us to engage in deep reflection, contemplation, and supplication, drawing us closer to God and seeking His intercession through the saints.

Throughout history, novenas have served as a means of expressing devotion, trust, and faith. They provide a structured framework for intense and continuous prayer, fostering a profound sense of spiritual communion and inviting the faithful to open their hearts to the grace and guidance of God. Novenas allow us to dedicate ourselves to a particular intention or seek the intercession of a specific saint, deepening our relationship with the divine and fostering a sense of hope and expectation.

Within the context of the novena devotion to St. Joseph, we enter into a unique and sacred journey. St. Joseph's powerful intercession has been witnessed by countless individuals throughout history, and the novena provides a dedicated space for us to seek his assistance and guidance in our lives. By dedicating nine days to prayer and contemplation, we open ourselves to the transformative power of St. Joseph's patronage and the abundant graces that flow through his intercession.

As we explore the history and significance of novenas, we will discover the rich spiritual heritage they hold. We will delve into the theological and practical aspects of this devotion, understanding how novenas connect us to the communion of saints, deepen our faith, and allow us to participate in the ongoing work of God's grace in our lives.

Through the exploration of the history and significance of novenas, we lay the foundation for our journey of devotion to St. Joseph. By embracing this powerful form of prayer, we are invited to experience the profound impact it can have on our spiritual lives. As we embark on this journey, may we open our hearts to the transformative power of the novena and allow St. Joseph's intercession to guide us closer to God, deepening our faith and enriching our relationship with the heavenly Father.

- St. Joseph: Patron Saint and Model of Faith

St. Joseph, the chosen foster father of Jesus and the spouse of the Blessed Virgin Mary, holds a prominent place as a patron saint and a model of faith within the Catholic Church. In this section, we delve into the life and virtues of St. Joseph, exploring his profound influence and significance in our spiritual journey.

St. Joseph's role as the guardian of the Holy Family exemplifies his unwavering faith and trust in God's plan. Chosen by divine providence to protect and nurture the Son of God, he faithfully embraced this extraordinary responsibility, demonstrating obedience and humility throughout his life. St. Joseph's unwavering trust in God's guidance serves as an inspiration for believers, showing us the power of surrendering our will to God and placing our trust in His providence.

As the earthly father of Jesus, St. Joseph played a pivotal role in salvation history. Despite the challenges and uncertainties he faced, he remained steadfast in his devotion to God and his commitment to fulfilling his role as the guardian and provider for Jesus and Mary. St. Joseph's example teaches us the importance of selflessness, sacrifice, and fidelity in our own lives, encouraging us to embrace our responsibilities and vocations with faith and dedication.

St. Joseph's silent presence in the Gospel narratives reflects his humility and humility. He willingly embraced a life of obscurity, focusing on fulfilling God's will rather than seeking personal acclaim or recognition. St. Joseph's humility teaches us the value of self-effacement and the importance of serving others without seeking recognition or reward.

Throughout his life, St. Joseph was a man of prayer and deep communion with God. His intimate relationship with the Father allowed him to discern God's will and respond with trust and obedience. St. Joseph's unwavering faith serves as a model for believers, urging us to cultivate a profound prayer life and seek God's guidance in all aspects of our lives.

As we delve into the novena devotion to St. Joseph, we draw inspiration from his virtues and seek to emulate his faith and trust in God. By embracing St. Joseph as our patron and model, we open ourselves to his intercession and guidance, inviting his presence and influence into our lives. Through the power of the novena, we seek to deepen our faith, strengthen our trust in God, and grow in holiness, following in the footsteps of this remarkable saint.

In the following chapters, we will explore how the novena devotion to St. Joseph can help us to cultivate these virtues and deepen our spiritual connection with him. By immersing ourselves in prayer, reflection, and contemplation, we embark on a transformative journey guided by the faith and example of St. Joseph. Together, let us seek his intercession and strive to become faithful disciples, entrusting our lives to the loving care of this esteemed patron saint.

Chapter 2: Understanding St. Joseph's Role in Salvation History

- St. Joseph: Chosen by God for a Divine Mission

In this chapter, we embark on a journey to explore the remarkable role that St. Joseph played in the grand tapestry of salvation history. As we delve into the circumstances surrounding his life and the divine mission entrusted to him, we gain a deeper appreciation for the significance and impact of St. Joseph's role in God's plan.

Imagine being chosen by God Himself for a mission of great importance. That was the reality that St. Joseph faced when he was handpicked to be the foster father of Jesus and the spouse of the Blessed Virgin Mary. It was no accident or coincidence; it was a divine appointment that spoke volumes about St. Joseph's character and unwavering faithfulness. Among all men, he was selected to fulfill the sacred duty of protecting and providing for the Son of God, ensuring His safety and well-being during His time on Earth.

The journey began with a whirlwind of emotions for St. Joseph. When he discovered Mary's pregnancy, he was undoubtedly perplexed and troubled. How could this be? But in the midst of his confusion, an angel appeared to him in a dream, revealing the truth of Mary's conception through the Holy Spirit. It was an extraordinary encounter that changed the course of St. Joseph's life forever.

In that moment, faced with a decision that would shape history, St. Joseph chose to heed the angel's message and embrace God's plan. With profound faith and humble obedience, he took Mary as his wife, accepting the role of a faithful protector and provider for the Holy Family. This act of trust and selflessness set the stage for St. Joseph's journey as a key figure in salvation history.

As the head of the Holy Family, St. Joseph's responsibilities went beyond the physical care of Jesus and Mary. He played a vital role in nurturing and guiding Jesus in His growth, both in His humanity and His spiritual development. St. Joseph, through his own example, instilled in Jesus the virtues of faith, obedience, and humility. He was a righteous man and a loving father, teaching Jesus life's lessons and preparing Him for His divine mission.

St. Joseph's unwavering faith and obedience to God's will continue to inspire believers today. In the face of personal challenges and sacrifices, he responded with immediate and complete surrender to God's plan. His example invites us to reflect on our own lives and consider how we can respond to God's call with unwavering trust and obedience.

By exploring St. Joseph's divine mission, we come to grasp the magnitude of his role in salvation history. Through his humble and selfless service, St. Joseph played an integral part in God's plan for the redemption of humanity. His presence and influence shaped the life of Jesus, contributing to His human upbringing and forming Him into the perfect example of love and obedience to the Father.

As we continue our journey of devotion to St. Joseph, we are invited to reflect on his role in salvation history and draw inspiration from his faithfulness. We can imagine the love and care that St. Joseph poured into his duties as the earthly father of Jesus, and we can seek to emulate his virtues in our own lives. Through the novena devotion to St. Joseph, we seek his intercession and guidance, allowing his virtues to shape our own spiritual journey. May we, like St. Joseph, respond to God's call with open hearts and unwavering faith, trusting in His divine plan for our lives.

- St. Joseph's Faith and Obedience

As we explore his deep trust in God and his willingness to submit to divine guidance, we gain a profound understanding of the virtues that made him a model for believers throughout the ages.

St. Joseph's faith was not a mere intellectual acknowledgment of God's existence; it was a living, active trust that permeated every aspect of his being. From the moment the angel appeared to him in a dream, St. Joseph's faith was put to the test. The news of Mary's pregnancy could have shattered his world and led him to doubt God's plan. Yet, in that crucial moment, he chose to believe, to place his confidence in the unseen workings of the Almighty.

With unyielding faith, St. Joseph embraced his role as the earthly father of Jesus, despite the questions and uncertainties that must have flooded his mind. He stepped forward with courage, accepting the responsibility entrusted to him by God. St. Joseph's faith enabled him to see beyond the ordinary and to recognize the extraordinary hand of God at work in his life and the life of his family.

It was through his unwavering obedience that St. Joseph demonstrated his deep trust in God's providence. When the angel instructed him to take Mary as his wife and to name the child Jesus, St. Joseph did not hesitate. He did not allow fear or human reasoning to hinder his obedience to the divine command. Instead, he humbly submitted himself to God's will, knowing that obedience to the heavenly Father was the path to true fulfillment.

St. Joseph's obedience extended beyond the initial encounter with the angel. Throughout his life, he continued to follow God's guidance with fidelity and devotion. From the journey to Bethlehem for the census to the flight into Egypt to protect the child Jesus from King Herod, St. Joseph's obedience was unwavering. He embraced the challenges and uncertainties with grace, trusting that God's wisdom far surpassed his own.

The faith and obedience of St. Joseph serve as an enduring example for all believers. In a world that often prioritizes self-reliance and personal agendas, St. Joseph's willingness to surrender his will to the divine will offers us a compelling model to follow. His faith reminds us that God's ways are higher than our ways and that true fulfillment lies in trusting and obeying Him.

Through the novena devotion to St. Joseph, we have the opportunity to cultivate the virtues of faith and obedience in our own lives. We can draw inspiration from St. Joseph's unwavering trust in God's plan, seeking to align our will with the divine will. As we deepen our faith and practice obedience in our daily lives, we open ourselves to the transformative power of God's grace, just as St. Joseph did.

In the following chapters, we will explore how the novena devotion to St. Joseph can help us strengthen our faith and nurture a spirit of obedience. By immersing ourselves in prayer, reflection, and contemplation, we embark on a transformative journey guided by the faith and example of St. Joseph. Together, let us seek his intercession and strive to become faithful disciples, entrusting our lives to the loving care of this esteemed patron saint.

- St. Joseph's Humility and Purity

Let us delve into the virtues of humility and purity that characterized the life of St. Joseph. As we explore his remarkable example of these virtues, we gain a deeper appreciation for their profound impact on his role in God's plan and their relevance in our own spiritual journey.

St. Joseph's humility was a hallmark of his character, evident in every aspect of his life. Despite being chosen by God for a divine mission, he never sought recognition or acclaim. Instead, he embraced a life of selflessness and service, content to fulfill his duties in the background. St. Joseph understood that true greatness lies not in exalting oneself but in humbly submitting to the will of God.

His humility was evident in the way he accepted his role as the foster father of Jesus. Despite being aware of Jesus' divine nature, St. Joseph did not assert his authority or demand recognition. Instead, he willingly took on the role of a humble and supportive guardian, providing for the needs of the Holy Family with love and devotion. His humility allowed him to play a crucial role in the upbringing of Jesus without seeking personal glory or praise.

St. Joseph's purity was also a distinguishing characteristic, exemplifying a life of moral integrity and holiness. As the spouse of the Blessed Virgin Mary, he lived a chaste and virtuous life, preserving the sanctity of their marriage and the sacredness of their union. His purity of heart and mind allowed him to fully embrace his role as the guardian of the Holy Family, fostering an environment of love, virtue, and grace.

In a world often consumed by self-gratification and moral compromise, St. Joseph's purity stands as a powerful example. His commitment to living a life of integrity reminds us of the importance of cultivating purity in our thoughts, words, and actions. St. Joseph invites us to reject the allure of worldly pleasures and instead pursue the path of virtue and holiness, recognizing that true joy and fulfillment come from aligning our lives with God's plan.

The humility and purity of St. Joseph are virtues that hold timeless significance for believers today. His example challenges us to examine our own lives and strive for greater humility in our interactions with others. We are called to let go of pride and self-centeredness, embracing a spirit of humility that allows us to serve and uplift those around us.

Likewise, St. Joseph's purity calls us to seek holiness in all aspects of our lives. It reminds us of the importance of safeguarding our hearts, minds, and bodies from the influences of impurity. By cultivating purity in our thoughts, words, and actions, we create a space within ourselves for God's grace to flow freely, transforming us from within.

Through the novena devotion to St. Joseph, we have the opportunity to embrace the virtues of humility and purity more fully. By reflecting on St. Joseph's example and seeking his intercession, we invite these virtues to take root in our lives. We ask for the grace to humbly serve others and to live lives of moral integrity, imitating St. Joseph's unwavering commitment to God's will.

As we continue our journey of devotion to St. Joseph, let us open our hearts to the transformative power of humility and purity. May these virtues shape our thoughts, guide our actions, and deepen our relationship with God and others. May St. Joseph, the humble and pure guardian of the Holy Family, intercede for us and lead us closer to the heart of Christ.

Chapter 3: Preparing for the Novena

- Setting the Stage for Prayer

In this chapter, we explore the importance of setting the stage for prayer as we embark on the journey of the novena devotion to St. Joseph. Just as we prepare a physical space for a special event or occasion, it is essential to create a sacred and conducive environment for our prayerful encounter with God through the intercession of St. Joseph.

The act of setting the stage for prayer involves intentionally creating an atmosphere that facilitates deep communion with God. It is a deliberate effort to carve out sacred space and time in the midst of our busy lives, allowing ourselves to enter into a place of quiet reflection, contemplation, and connection with the divine.

One way to set the stage for prayer is to find a physical space that serves as our sacred sanctuary. It could be a corner in our home, a quiet room, or even a dedicated prayer space adorned with religious images, icons, or candles. This designated space becomes a tangible reminder of our intention to encounter God and seek the intercession of St. Joseph during the novena.

As we prepare the physical space, we can also take steps to create an inner disposition of openness and receptivity. This involves cultivating an atmosphere of silence, stillness, and solitude, free from distractions that hinder our ability to focus on prayer. We may choose to disconnect from technology, turn off notifications, and create boundaries that protect this sacred time of communion with God.

Fasting and other spiritual practices can also play a role in setting the stage for prayer. By engaging in acts of self-discipline and detachment, we create space within ourselves to be more attuned to the promptings of the Holy Spirit. Fasting can help us detach from worldly attachments and desires, allowing us to enter into a state of humility, reliance on God, and deeper spiritual awareness.

Additionally, incorporating rituals or symbolic actions can enhance our preparation for prayer.

Lighting a candle, reciting a specific prayer or mantra, or engaging in simple acts of purification can serve as reminders of our intention and create a sense of sacredness in our hearts.

In setting the stage for prayer, we acknowledge that our encounter with God through the novena to St. Joseph is not a casual or routine activity. It is a deliberate and intentional pursuit of communion with the divine. By creating a sacred space, fostering silence and stillness, practicing self-discipline, and engaging in meaningful rituals, we open ourselves to the transformative power of prayer and the intercession of St. Joseph.

As we embark on this journey, let us prepare our hearts and minds to enter into deeper communion with God. Let us set aside dedicated time and space, free from distractions, to cultivate an atmosphere of prayer. May our preparation for the novena be a reflection of our sincere desire to encounter God and seek the intercession of St. Joseph, allowing his guidance and presence to permeate every aspect of our lives.

- Creating a Sacred Space

Just as physical surroundings can influence our state of mind and emotions, intentionally crafting a sacred space can enhance our prayer experience and foster a deeper connection with God and St. Joseph.

Creating a sacred space is an invitation to transform a physical location into a place of encounter with the divine. It is a deliberate act of setting apart a specific area or room and infusing it with elements that evoke a sense of reverence, peace, and spiritual focus. By doing so, we create a tangible space that supports and enhances our prayerful journey.

One way to create a sacred space is by choosing a designated area for prayer within our home. It could be a quiet corner, a room, or even a small table adorned with religious items such as statues, icons, or sacred images of St. Joseph. These visual reminders serve as points of focus and inspiration, drawing our attention to the presence of God and St. Joseph during our novena prayers.

Consider decorating the space with elements that evoke a sense of tranquility and sacredness. Soft lighting, candles, or incense can create an atmosphere of calm and reverence. Incorporating natural elements like plants, flowers, or a small water fountain can further enhance the ambiance and remind us of the beauty and wonder of God's creation.

Personalize the sacred space with items that hold deep meaning or significance to you. It could be a cherished religious object, a journal for reflection, or a collection of prayers and devotional materials. By including these personal touches, we infuse the space with our own spiritual journey, making it uniquely ours.

In addition to physical objects, consider incorporating auditory elements to enhance the sacred space. Soft instrumental music, Gregorian chants, or recordings of sacred hymns can create a soothing and prayerful atmosphere. The gentle melodies can help calm our minds, elevate our spirits, and facilitate a deeper sense of connection with God and St. Joseph.

Creating a sacred space is not limited to our physical surroundings; it extends to our internal disposition as well. As we enter the sacred space, it is essential to cultivate an attitude of reverence, openness, and attentiveness. We can prepare our hearts through a moment of silence, deep breathing, or a simple prayer, inviting the Holy Spirit to guide our thoughts and intentions throughout the novena.

By intentionally creating a sacred space, we invite God's presence and St. Joseph's intercession into our prayerful journey. It becomes a sanctuary where we can seek solace, guidance, and inspiration. As we enter this sacred space, we open ourselves to the transformative power of God's love and the profound impact of St. Joseph's intercession in our lives.

May our sacred spaces be a haven where we can pour out our hearts, share our joys and struggles, and deepen our relationship with God and St. Joseph. May they be places where we find solace, strength, and renewal as we embark on the novena devotion. Let us honor these sacred spaces as tangible reminders of our commitment to prayer and our desire to draw closer to the heart of God through the powerful intercession of St. Joseph.

- Fasting and Other Spiritual Practices

In this section, we explore the significance of fasting and other spiritual practices as integral parts of our preparation for the novena devotion to St. Joseph. These practices serve as powerful tools to deepen our spiritual connection, cultivate discipline, and open ourselves to the transformative power of prayer.

Fasting, as a spiritual practice, involves willingly abstaining from food or certain types of food for a specific period. It is a time-honored tradition observed by many religious traditions as a means of self-discipline, purification, and spiritual focus. By voluntarily limiting our physical nourishment, we redirect our attention and energy towards the spiritual realm.

During the novena to St. Joseph, fasting can serve as a tangible expression of our devotion and commitment. It allows us to detach from the distractions of our physical appetites and turn our hearts and minds towards God. In this state of physical hunger, we become more attuned to our spiritual hunger, seeking a deeper encounter with God and a greater reliance on His grace.

While fasting, it is important to approach it with a spirit of intentionality and reverence. We can use this time to reflect on the virtues of St. Joseph and the example he sets for us. We can offer our sacrifices as acts of solidarity with those who hunger for physical or spiritual nourishment, and as an expression of gratitude for the blessings we have received.

In addition to fasting, there are other spiritual practices that can complement our preparation for the novena. These practices can include acts of charity, such as serving others in need, volunteering, or donating to charitable causes. Engaging in acts of love and selflessness aligns us with the virtues of St. Joseph and prepares our hearts to receive the graces of the novena.

Prayer and scripture reading are foundational spiritual practices that should not be overlooked. Setting aside dedicated time each day to engage in heartfelt prayer, whether it be through reciting traditional prayers, spontaneous dialogue with God, or meditative contemplation, allows us to deepen our connection with the divine and seek the intercession of St. Joseph. Likewise, immersing ourselves in the Word of God through the reading and reflection of scripture opens our hearts and minds to receive divine guidance and inspiration.

Lastly, cultivating an attitude of gratitude and thanksgiving is a powerful spiritual practice. By expressing gratitude for the blessings in our lives and recognizing God's providence, we shift our focus from what is lacking to what is abundant. Gratitude opens our hearts to receive the abundant graces and blessings that flow from our novena devotion to St. Joseph.

As we prepare for the novena, let us embrace the spiritual practices of fasting, acts of charity, prayer, scripture reading, and gratitude. These practices deepen our connection with God, purify our intentions, and prepare us to receive the transformative power of the novena. May they serve as stepping stones on our spiritual journey and draw us closer to the heart of St. Joseph, who exemplified these virtues in his own life.

Chapter 4: Unveiling the Nine-Day Novena

- Day 1: Praying for Faith and Trust

We begin this prayer, In the name of the Father, and of the Son, and of the Holy Spirit. Amen.

Oh, St. Joseph, whose defense before God's throne is so vast, so powerful, and so swift. I put all my interests and ambitions in you. (**Say your intentions here.**)

Oh St. Joseph, please help me by your mighty intercession and secure for me all spiritual benefits from your divine Son through Jesus Christ, our Lord. To be able to express my gratitude and adoration to the most loving of Fathers after having engaged here under your heavenly influence.

Oh, St. Joseph, I never get tired of thinking about you and Jesus resting in your arms. I dare not approach when He is lying close to your heart.

When I'm about to take my last breath, beg him to kiss His beautiful head in my honor and reciprocate the kiss.

St. Joseph, Patron of departing souls – Pray for me.

Say 1: Our Father...Say 1: Hail Mary...Say 1: Glory Be...

- Day 2: Seeking St. Joseph's Intercession for Families

We begin this prayer, In the name of the Father, and of the Son, and of the Holy Spirit. Amen.

Oh, St. Joseph, whose defense before God's throne is so vast, so powerful, and so swift. I put all my interests and ambitions in you. (**Say your intentions here**.)

Oh St. Joseph, please help me by your mighty intercession and secure for me all spiritual benefits from your divine Son through Jesus Christ, our Lord. To be able to express my gratitude and adoration to the most loving of Fathers after having engaged here under your heavenly influence.

Oh, St. Joseph, I never get tired of thinking about you and Jesus resting in your arms. I dare not approach when He is lying close to your heart. When I'm about to take my last breath, beg him to kiss His beautiful head in my honor and reciprocate the kiss.

St. Joseph, Patron of departing souls – Pray for me.

Say 1: Our Father...Say 1: Hail Mary...Say 1: Glory Be...

- Day 3: Embracing St. Joseph as the Patron of Workers

We begin this prayer, In the name of the Father, and of the Son, and of the Holy Spirit. Amen.

Oh, St. Joseph, whose defense before God's throne is so vast, so powerful, and so swift. I put all my interests and ambitions in you. (**Say your intentions here**.)

Oh St. Joseph, please help me by your mighty intercession and secure for me all spiritual benefits from your divine Son through Jesus Christ, our Lord. To be able to express my gratitude and adoration to the most loving of Fathers after having engaged here under your heavenly influence.

Oh, St. Joseph, I never get tired of thinking about you and Jesus resting in your arms. I dare not approach when He is lying close to your heart. When I'm about to take my last breath, beg him to kiss His beautiful head in my honor and reciprocate the kiss.

St. Joseph, Patron of departing souls – Pray for me.

Say 1: Our Father…Say 1: Hail Mary…Say 1: Glory Be…

- Day 4: Finding Comfort in St. Joseph's Guidance

We begin this prayer, In the name of the Father, and of the Son, and of the Holy Spirit. Amen.

Oh, St. Joseph, whose defense before God's throne is so vast, so powerful, and so swift. I put all my interests and ambitions in you. (**Say your intentions here**.)

Oh St. Joseph, please help me by your mighty intercession and secure for me all spiritual benefits from your divine Son through Jesus Christ, our Lord. To be able to express my gratitude and adoration to the most loving of Fathers after having engaged here under your heavenly influence.

Oh, St. Joseph, I never get tired of thinking about you and Jesus resting in your arms. I dare not approach when He is lying close to your heart. When I'm about to take my last breath, beg him to kiss His beautiful head in my honor and reciprocate the kiss.

St. Joseph, Patron of departing souls – Pray for me.

Say 1: Our Father...Say 1: Hail Mary...Say 1: Glory Be...

- Day 5: Seeking St. Joseph's Help in Times of Difficulty

We begin this prayer, In the name of the Father, and of the Son, and of the Holy Spirit. Amen.

Oh, St. Joseph, whose defense before God's throne is so vast, so powerful, and so swift. I put all my interests and ambitions in you. (**Say your intentions here.**)

Oh St. Joseph, please help me by your mighty intercession and secure for me all spiritual benefits from your divine Son through Jesus Christ, our Lord. To be able to express my gratitude and adoration to the most loving of Fathers after having engaged here under your heavenly influence.

Oh, St. Joseph, I never get tired of thinking about you and Jesus resting in your arms. I dare not approach when He is lying close to your heart. When I'm about to take my last breath, beg him to kiss His beautiful head in my honor and reciprocate the kiss.

St. Joseph, Patron of departing souls – Pray for me.

Say 1: Our Father…Say 1: Hail Mary…Say 1: Glory Be…

- Day 6: Praying for Purity and Chastity

We begin this prayer, In the name of the Father, and of the Son, and of the Holy Spirit. Amen.

Oh, St. Joseph, whose defense before God's throne is so vast, so powerful, and so swift. I put all my interests and ambitions in you. (**Say your intentions here.**)

Oh St. Joseph, please help me by your mighty intercession and secure for me all spiritual benefits from your divine Son through Jesus Christ, our Lord. To be able to express my gratitude and adoration to the most loving of Fathers after having engaged here under your heavenly influence.

Oh, St. Joseph, I never get tired of thinking about you and Jesus resting in your arms. I dare not approach when He is lying close to your heart. When I'm about to take my last breath, beg him to kiss His beautiful head in my honor and reciprocate the kiss.

St. Joseph, Patron of departing souls – Pray for me.

Say 1: Our Father...Say 1: Hail Mary...Say 1: Glory Be...

- Day 7: St. Joseph as a Model of Silence and Contemplation

We begin this prayer, In the name of the Father, and of the Son, and of the Holy Spirit. Amen.

Oh, St. Joseph, whose defense before God's throne is so vast, so powerful, and so swift. I put all my interests and ambitions in you. (**Say your intentions here**.)

Oh St. Joseph, please help me by your mighty intercession and secure for me all spiritual benefits from your divine Son through Jesus Christ, our Lord. To be able to express my gratitude and adoration to the most loving of Fathers after having engaged here under your heavenly influence.

Oh, St. Joseph, I never get tired of thinking about you and Jesus resting in your arms. I dare not approach when He is lying close to your heart. When I'm about to take my last breath, beg him to kiss His beautiful head in my honor and reciprocate the kiss.

St. Joseph, Patron of departing souls – Pray for me.

Say 1: Our Father…Say 1: Hail Mary…Say 1: Glory Be…

- Day 8: St. Joseph's Intercession for the Dying

We begin this prayer, In the name of the Father, and of the Son, and of the Holy Spirit. Amen.

Oh, St. Joseph, whose defense before God's throne is so vast, so powerful, and so swift. I put all my interests and ambitions in you. (**Say your intentions here**.)

Oh St. Joseph, please help me by your mighty intercession and secure for me all spiritual benefits from your divine Son through Jesus Christ, our Lord. To be able to express my gratitude and adoration to the most loving of Fathers after having engaged here under your heavenly influence.

Oh, St. Joseph, I never get tired of thinking about you and Jesus resting in your arms. I dare not approach when He is lying close to your heart. When I'm about to take my last breath, beg him to kiss His beautiful head in my honor and reciprocate the kiss.

St. Joseph, Patron of departing souls – Pray for me.

Say 1: Our Father...Say 1: Hail Mary...Say 1: Glory Be...

- Day 9: Celebrating St. Joseph's Glorious Patronage

We begin this prayer, In the name of the Father, and of the Son, and of the Holy Spirit. Amen.

Oh, St. Joseph, whose defense before God's throne is so vast, so powerful, and so swift. I put all my interests and ambitions in you. (**Say your intentions here**.)

Oh St. Joseph, please help me by your mighty intercession and secure for me all spiritual benefits from your divine Son through Jesus Christ, our Lord. To be able to express my gratitude and adoration to the most loving of Fathers after having engaged here under your heavenly influence.

Oh, St. Joseph, I never get tired of thinking about you and Jesus resting in your arms. I dare not approach when He is lying close to your heart. When I'm about to take my last breath, beg him to kiss His beautiful head in my honor and reciprocate the kiss.

St. Joseph, Patron of departing souls – Pray for me.

Say 1: Our Father...Say 1: Hail Mary...Say 1: Glory Be...

Saint Joseph Prayer of Protection

"Great St. Joseph,
I trust you with all of my interests and desires because of your powerful and swift protection before the Throne of God. In the name of our Lord and Savior, Jesus Christ, please help me by making the strongest possible intercession on my behalf. I also give gratitude to God, the most loving of Fathers, and do him reverence by obtaining here below your Heavenly favor.

I never get tired of seeing you, Great St. Joseph, holding the sleeping Jesus Child.

When I take my last breath, please ask for His love's favor for me!

St. Joseph, the Patron of
departing souls — Pray for me."

Powerful Prayer to St. Joseph

"Saint Joseph,

I humbly ask Thee to keep me free from all uncleanness and to grant that my mind, heart, and body may all be kept pure; enable me constantly to serve Jesus and Mary in perfect chastity. I do this through Jesus and Mary, two vows so precious to you. Father and protector of virgins, to whose devoted care Innocence itself was committed, together with Christ Jesus and Mary, the Virgin of virgins.

Amen."

Chapter 5: Testimonials and Miraculous Stories

- Real-life Experiences of St. Joseph's Intercession

Maria's Journey of Healing

Maria, a devoted Catholic, had been suffering from a chronic illness for many years. Despite seeking various medical treatments, her condition seemed to worsen over time, leaving her feeling hopeless and discouraged. Desperate for relief, Maria turned to St. Joseph, imploring his intercession for healing.

With unwavering faith, Maria began a novena dedicated to St. Joseph, fervently praying for his intervention. As the days passed, Maria felt a sense of peace and reassurance enveloping her. She continued to entrust her health to St. Joseph, firmly believing in his loving care.

One evening, while in prayer, Maria experienced a profound moment of spiritual consolation. She felt a warm, gentle presence surrounding her, and a deep sense of healing washed over her body. From that moment forward, Maria's health started to improve steadily. Medical tests revealed unexpected positive changes, and doctors were astounded by her progress.

Maria attributes her healing to the powerful intercession of St. Joseph. She continues to offer prayers of gratitude, sharing her testimony of St. Joseph's miraculous intercession with others, encouraging them to place their trust in his loving care.

John's Financial Miracle

John, a hardworking father of three, faced overwhelming financial difficulties. His business had been struggling for years, and the burden of mounting debts seemed insurmountable. Feeling defeated and on the verge of bankruptcy, John turned to St. Joseph, the patron of workers, for assistance.

With a humble heart, John began a dedicated novena to St. Joseph, seeking his intercession for financial relief. He placed his business and financial worries into the hands of St. Joseph, entrusting him with his family's future.

In the midst of his novena, an unexpected turn of events occurred. A long-lost client, whom John hadn't heard from in years, reached out with a significant business opportunity. The contract not only saved John's struggling business but also brought a newfound stability and growth that he had long prayed for.

John firmly believes that this turnaround was a direct result of St. Joseph's intercession. He continues to honor St. Joseph in his daily life, recognizing him as a faithful guide and protector in times of financial distress.

The Reconciliation of Sarah's Family

Sarah had carried the heavy burden of a broken family relationship for years. A deep divide had formed between her and her sibling, causing immense pain and estrangement. Despite attempts at reconciliation, the wounds seemed irreparable, leaving Sarah devastated.

Seeking a miraculous healing of her family, Sarah turned to St. Joseph, known for his role as a protector of families. With a heart full of hope, she embarked on a dedicated novena, praying for St. Joseph's intercession to mend the broken bonds and restore familial love.

During the novena, Sarah experienced a remarkable transformation within her family. Walls of bitterness and resentment began to crumble, and opportunities for open communication and forgiveness arose. Slowly but surely, reconciliation took place, bringing healing and unity to their fractured relationship.

Sarah attributes this miraculous turnaround to the powerful intercession of St. Joseph. She now cherishes the renewed bond with her sibling and continues to nurture their relationship with love and gratitude, knowing that it was St. Joseph's intercession that brought about this miraculous reconciliation.

These testimonials stand as a testament to the powerful intercession of St. Joseph. They reveal the profound impact he can have on the lives of those who turn to him with faith and trust. Through his loving care and intervention, miracles unfold, bringing healing, provision, and reconciliation. May these stories inspire others to seek the intercession of St. Joseph and experience his miraculous power in their own lives.

Laura's Journey to Motherhood

Laura and her husband had been struggling with infertility for several years, longing to conceive a child of their own. They had undergone numerous medical treatments and consultations, but their hopes of starting a family seemed dim. In their despair, Laura turned to St. Joseph, the guardian and protector of the Holy Family, for his intercession.

With fervent prayers and unwavering faith, Laura embarked on a special novena dedicated to St. Joseph, entrusting him with their deepest desire to become parents. She poured her heart out to St. Joseph, seeking his guidance and assistance in this challenging journey.

Months later, to their immense joy and surprise, Laura discovered that she was pregnant. It was a miraculous turn of events that defied all medical expectations. The couple celebrated this precious gift of life, acknowledging St. Joseph's intercession as the source of their blessing.

Laura firmly believes that St. Joseph's powerful intercession played a pivotal role in their journey to parenthood. She continues to hold a special place in her heart for St. Joseph, recognizing him as a loving father who listens to the cries of his children and blesses them with abundant grace.

Mark's Journey of Spiritual Transformation

Mark had been leading a life consumed by material pursuits and worldly ambitions, feeling empty and unfulfilled. Despite his accomplishments, he yearned for deeper meaning and purpose. Seeking spiritual guidance and a transformation of heart, Mark turned to St. Joseph, the epitome of humility and purity.

With a sincere desire for change, Mark embarked on a spiritual journey, incorporating devotion to St. Joseph into his daily life. He prayed for St. Joseph's intercession to purify his heart, guide him towards a life of virtue, and deepen his relationship with God.

As the days and weeks passed, Mark experienced a profound inner transformation. He felt a renewed sense of purpose and a deepened connection to his faith. The worldly attachments that once held him captive began to lose their grip, making room for a more meaningful and spiritually fulfilling life.

Mark attributes this remarkable transformation to the powerful intercession of St. Joseph. He continues to rely on St. Joseph's guidance and looks to him as a role model of faith, humility, and purity. Mark's journey serves as an inspiration to others seeking a spiritual transformation and a deeper relationship with God.

As you reflect on these accounts, may they inspire you to turn to St. Joseph in your own trials and challenges. Whether you seek physical healing, financial stability, familial harmony, or spiritual growth, may these stories instill in you a renewed hope and trust in the intercession of St. Joseph. Allow his loving guidance to accompany you on your own journey of faith and experience the transformative power of his intercession in your life.

Chapter 6: Strengthening Your Devotion to St. Joseph

- Incorporating St. Joseph into Daily Life

St. Joseph, the Patron Saint of the Universal Church, offers us a remarkable example of faith, humility, and obedience. As we deepen our devotion to him, it is essential to find ways to incorporate St. Joseph into our daily lives, allowing his presence and influence to shape our thoughts, actions, and relationships.

In this Chapter, we explore practical ways to strengthen our connection with St. Joseph and make him an integral part of our everyday routines. By inviting St. Joseph into our lives, we open ourselves to his intercession, guidance, and inspiration, drawing closer to his virtuous example and deepening our relationship with him as a spiritual father and protector.

One way to incorporate St. Joseph into daily life is through morning prayers. As we begin our day, we can consciously invoke St. Joseph's intercession, entrusting our intentions, plans, and challenges to his care. By placing our trust in him, we invite his wisdom and guidance to accompany us throughout the day, seeking his intercession in all our endeavors.

Another way to honor St. Joseph is by seeking his intercession in our work life. St. Joseph is not only the Patron Saint of Workers but also a model of diligence, integrity, and dedication. By emulating his virtues in our professional lives, we bring honor to God and contribute to the well-being of others. We can pray to St. Joseph for guidance and assistance in our work, asking him to intercede for success, integrity, and fulfillment in our vocational pursuits.

Praying the Litany of St. Joseph is a beautiful way to deepen our devotion and understanding of his role in salvation history. The litany encompasses the various titles, virtues, and attributes associated with St. Joseph, allowing us to meditate on his life and character. By incorporating the litany into our prayer routine, we honor St. Joseph's unique role and seek his intercession with a greater appreciation for his virtues.

In addition to specific practices, incorporating St. Joseph into daily life also involves embracing his virtues and imitating his example. St. Joseph's faith, humility, obedience, and selflessness are qualities that we can strive to embody in our interactions with others and our relationship with God. By cultivating these virtues, we not only honor St. Joseph but also grow in holiness and become better disciples of Christ.

As we seek to incorporate St. Joseph into our daily lives, let us remember that our devotion to him is not limited to prayers and rituals alone. It is a call to embrace his virtues, to model our lives after his example, and to seek his intercession in all aspects of our existence. By inviting St. Joseph into our daily routines, we invite his fatherly love and guidance, experiencing the transformative power of his presence in our lives.

May our efforts to incorporate St. Joseph into our daily lives deepen our devotion to him, strengthen our faith, and draw us closer to the heart of Jesus.

May St. Joseph, the silent guardian of the Holy Family, intercede for us and lead us on the path of holiness, guiding us to become true disciples and faithful children of God.

- Living the Virtues of St. Joseph

St. Joseph, the earthly father of Jesus and the spouse of the Blessed Virgin Mary, is revered for his exemplary virtues. As we deepen our devotion to St. Joseph, it is essential to not only seek his intercession but also strive to live out the virtues that he embodied.

In this section, we explore the virtues of St. Joseph and how we can incorporate them into our own lives. By embracing these virtues, we not only honor St. Joseph but also grow in holiness and become better disciples of Christ.

1. Faith: St. Joseph's unwavering faith in God's plan is an inspiration to us all. He trusted in God's guidance, even in the face of uncertainty and difficulty. To live the virtue of faith like St. Joseph, we can cultivate a deep trust in God's providence, surrendering our worries and fears to Him. We can seek to deepen our relationship with God through prayer, Scripture study, and participation in the sacraments.

2. Humility: St. Joseph's humility is evident in his willingness to accept his role as the foster father of Jesus, despite his own limitations and insignificance in the eyes of the world. To live the virtue of humility like St. Joseph, we can strive to recognize our own dependence on God, embracing a posture of gratitude and service. We can humbly accept our strengths and weaknesses, using our talents to build up others rather than seeking recognition or praise.

3. Obedience: St. Joseph's immediate and complete obedience to God's commands is a testament to his trust and love for the Lord. He followed God's guidance without hesitation, even when it required sacrifice and uncertainty. To live the virtue of obedience like St. Joseph, we can strive to align our will with God's will, surrendering our desires and submitting to His plan for our lives. We can listen attentively to His voice in prayer and discernment, responding with openness and willingness to follow His lead.

4. Purity: St. Joseph's purity of heart and mind made him a worthy guardian of the Holy Family. He embraced a life of chastity and virtue, demonstrating self-control and reverence in his thoughts, words, and actions. To live the virtue of purity like St. Joseph, we can strive for moral integrity, guarding our hearts and minds from impurity and seeking to live out God's plan for human sexuality. We can foster a culture of purity in our relationships, media choices, and personal habits, honoring the dignity of ourselves and others.

5. Patience: St. Joseph's patient endurance in the midst of challenges and uncertainties is an example of steadfastness and trust. He embraced the hidden years of his life, faithfully fulfilling his responsibilities as the protector and provider for Jesus and Mary. To live the virtue of patience like St. Joseph, we can cultivate a spirit of perseverance, trusting in God's timing and providence. We can patiently bear the difficulties and trials that come our way, relying on God's grace to sustain us.

By consciously striving to live out these virtues, we not only honor St. Joseph but also grow in holiness and draw closer to Christ. As we incorporate the virtues of faith, humility, obedience, purity, and patience into our lives, we become more effective witnesses of God's love and grace in the world.

May St. Joseph, the humble and faithful guardian of the Holy Family, intercede for us and help us to imitate his virtues. May his example inspire us to deepen our devotion to him and to live out these virtues in our daily lives, becoming true disciples of Christ and bringing His light to the world.

Conclusion: Embracing the Everlasting Power of the Novena to St. Joseph

Throughout this book, we have embarked on a journey of discovering the power and significance of the Novena devotion to St. Joseph. We have explored the history and significance of novenas, delved into St. Joseph's role as the patron saint and model of faith, and learned how to prepare ourselves for this beautiful nine-day prayer practice.

We have witnessed the profound impact of St. Joseph's intercession in the lives of individuals, families, and communities. Real-life experiences and miraculous stories have testified to the power of St. Joseph's intervention and his loving care for those who seek his help.

As we have ventured through the chapters, we have also discovered ways to strengthen our devotion to St. Joseph. We have learned to incorporate him into our daily lives, seeking his guidance and intercession in our prayers, work, and relationships. We have strived to emulate his virtues of faith, humility, obedience, purity, and patience, recognizing him as a model and inspiration for our own spiritual journey.

The Novena to St. Joseph is not just a series of prayers or a ritual to be performed mechanically. It is a pathway to encounter the ever-present love and power of St. Joseph, a means to draw closer to his heart and to experience the transformative grace of his intercession. The novena opens a door to a deeper relationship with St. Joseph, inviting us to entrust our needs, joys, and sorrows to his fatherly care.

As we conclude this book, let us continue to embrace the everlasting power of the Novena to St. Joseph in our lives. Let us persevere in prayer, placing our trust in St. Joseph's loving intercession, knowing that he is a faithful and compassionate patron who desires to help us on our journey of faith.

May the devotion to St. Joseph strengthen our relationship with God and deepen our love for Jesus and Mary. May it inspire us to imitate St. Joseph's virtues and to live lives of faith, humility, obedience, purity, and patience. May St. Joseph, the guardian and protector of the Holy Family, intercede for us and lead us closer to the heart of God.

With St. Joseph as our guide and companion, let us continue to walk in faith, entrusting ourselves to his loving care, and experiencing the grace and blessings that flow from this powerful novena devotion. May our devotion to St. Joseph bring us ever closer to the heart of God and enrich our lives with His abundant love and mercy.

In the words of St. Joseph, let us say, "Jesus, Mary, and Joseph, I give you my heart and my soul." May our devotion to St. Joseph transform our lives and draw us deeper into the divine mysteries of our faith.

Amen.

Printed in Great Britain
by Amazon

43031998R00046